The crystals reflect delicacy, transparency, and brightness and will become firmly connected to a series of links, thereby converting them into an indestructible chain.

They were made under pressure and are amorphous but can become brittle in the face of the decision to think and act differently.

Crystal Chains

IN THE WORKPLACE

Angela Cook
&
Cristina Monroy

BALBOA.
PRESS

A DIVISION OF HAY HOUSE

Author Credits: Cover design by Maria Paula Fonseca

Balboa Press books may be ordered through booksellers or by contacting:

Balboa Press
A Division of Hay House
1663 Liberty Drive
Bloomington, IN 47403
www.balboapress.com
1 (877) 407-4847

Print information available on the last page.

ISBN: 978-1-5043-8031-7 (sc)
ISBN: 978-1-5043-8032-4 (e)

Library of Congress Control Number: 2017907377

Balboa Press rev. date: 05/17/2017

Contents

Introduction

Someone told me in secret that the
only person who could break the
crystal chains that bind me is me!

As human beings, we know of the importance of the different areas of our lives—that is, professional, personal, spiritual, academic, and so on.

We grow up with the norms, beliefs, and teachings that our parents gave us in the beginning with their words and examples. They guided us according to what they had learned in their development. They taught us by doing what was for them correct, with the goal of giving us only the best of everything.

Eventually, we began to assume roles for which the majority of us were ill prepared, and this is when we realized we had lost innate qualities, such as spontaneity and creativity. Additionally, we created some limitations, such as shyness, insecurity, and submissiveness. These traits can generate and develop unimaginable bonds, that I called crystal chains. These are formed mentally and in different stages of our lives. They bind us and lead us to unconsciously act against our best wishes.

Crystal chains can be broken, which generates changes in our thinking, words, and actions. This can lead us to face circumstances differently and to look ahead and solve what is presented to us.

If we make a choice, we can make it our mission. We will get the results we want. It is simply a matter of believing in what we do, doing it well, and growing with our plans, even changing them a thousand times if necessary while remaining helpful and respectful.

In Crystal Chains: In the Workplace, you will find different business situations where challenges are presented that can affect your development in this area of your life. However, through recognition, acceptance, and good decisions, we can make the chains fragile, like crystal, and break them, resulting in our personal growth. Being in the present moment gives us the possibility of living better in all aspects of our lives.

The following narrative reveals, with colloquial examples, scenarios of daily living in the organizational environment and the roles we play in our work. In addition, it points to the importance of understanding that the company where we work includes all of us. We want to succeed and be heard. We are creative beings, and by respecting ourselves, we achieve the best relationships with each other.

The series of Crystal Chains books will show you how to generate that personal change that will help you in the different areas of your life and will allow you to break the chains that you might currently possess. Either way, you are free to make decisions.

Chapter 1

Getting To Know Ourselves

• Assuming Control

It should be clear to everyone that companies are run by people; that each of us plays a different role within them; and, depending on how we play, we win or lose.

We also know that all companies seek to be leaders in their sectors, which are influenced by markets so competitive that they must change quickly over time if they want to succeed.

These changes are dependent on each and every one of us participating in our companies' success to the extent that we join efforts in pursuit of the same objectives.

If these changes do not happen and if we, as leaders in our organizations, do not change, companies simply need to close their doors.

- **Identifying Us at Work**

  Knowing ourselves can easily help us identify what we really want to do for work.

  Knowing our qualities, limitations, abilities to adapt, and professional levels determines how we relate to others. If we are truly contributing our knowledge and ideas, opportunities will arise within our companies to learn and develop on many other levels.

  Some questions that we can ask are: What do I really want to do? What is my knowledge level? What are the opportunities I have at work?

  It is valuable to stop and look at what we are doing with our lives, to learn more about ourselves and reinforce our relationship with ourselves.

  Many times, we analyze our lives, critique ourselves, doubt our abilities, and become discouraged, and our behavior is not in accordance with what we want to achieve. Other times, we give more importance to the opinions of others, letting those opinions have more value than our own.

  This doesn't mean that it's not good to listen and evaluate what is right for us. We must be clear, however, about who we are and where we are going, because the images we project may be different from who we really are, and the people around us may not see our true selves. They create their own images of us, possibly wrong, and this is an influential factor in our interpersonal relationships.

Only on a few occasions do we make a positive self-critique, but when we do, we usually change our perspectives, look at ourselves, and become aware of what we want to change and how far we want to reach in all aspects of our lives. This self-knowledge analysis is of vital importance for our work development.

- **Satisfaction = Productivity**

We assume commitments when we freely decide to work for a company that compensates us for the work we perform.

Each of us has developed different qualities—some more than others—such as listening and communication skills, creativity, patience, and organization. We are responsible for and must manage our assigned tasks by applying the above and other leadership qualities that we innately have but sometimes don't recognize.

The satisfaction we feel in our work can only be experienced by us. Many times, another person doing the same work may feel better about it or may seem bored or uninterested. It is healthy to evaluate and know if we are satisfied with the role we play.

If we clearly identify ourselves in our roles and feel happy about what we do, it will be reflected in every aspect of our lives.

- **Decision: Tranquility**

  For the majority, we ourselves are the ones who make the decision to accept a job.

  We begin to work at a company with great expectations in the position that they have offered us and with a desire to progress. Over time, we may see that the position, conditions, way of working, responsibilities, and/or the work is not what we imagined or is not meeting our expectations. Therefore, it is time to make a decision.

  If you decide to continue with this work, then make the best of it—you already know that you can manage your position. If your decision is to look for a new opportunity, then do it; don't let crystal chains form around you that, over time, are difficult to break.

Leave this work with the same gratitude as the day you accepted the position. You'll be giving the option to another person with expectations different from your own. He or she will occupy that position and possibly get better. This will benefit the person and the company.

Let's remember that we create our world. Every moment in our lives is valuable, and regardless of the work we are performing, it must give us one of the most precious gifts in life: our tranquility (peace of mind).

Chapter 2

With Love

- ## The Feeling

    We have heard and spoken during our lives the word love; we use it to show others all kinds of affection and feelings that we have inside. Over time, you have probably seen that these feelings we call love are magical and lead us to do what we may have believed to be impossible. This magic can be the foundation for all areas of our lives.

- ## A Step Toward Success

    The lives of thousands of people focus on their workplaces. Also, we can't ignore the fact that many of us have daily tasks in addition to work. These might include caring for the family, shopping, cooking, and cleaning, to name a few.

If we look at how a normal day develops, we can conclude the following: everything starts from the moment we prepare for work. We organize the clothes that we are going to wear (some do it the night before); set the alarm; rise in the morning and get cleaned up; eat breakfast; get dressed; prepare snacks, if we desire, to eat during breaks at work; and finally, drive to or go out and wait for our rides to work. We conduct our work at the company and, when we finish, return home and repeat something similar to the above day after day.

If we add up all the time we invest in the ritual of going to and coming from our work, plus the time we spend at work, we can clearly see that it is the area where we spend most of our time.

I ask myself, Do I do all this as an obligation? Is it a routine? Is this what I really want? Is this something I must do, or is it done with love?

We all want to be successful and have tranquility in what we undertake, even in our work. When we start a new job, we do it with the desire to be successful. I don't think any of us want mediocre results. Accepting mediocrity would give us feelings of rejection or loss, and this would not bring fulfillment to our lives.

- **Innate Motivation**

  For all of us, it is important to do our jobs well. When we do them with love, we feel peace, harmony, and joy, and work is more pleasant. When we live in the present moment, we handle situations more easily. When we don't live in the present moment, we rob ourselves of the patience needed to accomplish things with a high level of motivation. This motivation is innate, and with it, we can achieve any goals that we undertake.

  On the other hand, the results may be very different if we perform that same job angrily, grumpily, reluctantly, lazily, or with stress.

- **Solution Builder**

  Let's analyze what happens when we attempt to solve a situation using a feeling different from serenity, tranquility, or love, such as anger. A bad mood makes analyzing a problem more complicated, and the solution may come more slowly and may not be what we expected. We make more mistakes. We sometimes even mistreat other people with our words or actions. We can't resolve the situation because we lose objectivity when performing the analysis.

However, if the situation is seen from the perspective of love, all of the possible solutions may be revealed more clearly.

● A Matter Of Attitude

In some cases, a self-image and a certain attitude toward others causes them to believe that we are in the lead or in command, and we believe that we must be at all times serious, stressed, and moody. We might give inaccurate answers, making others believe that we are actually producing more than 100 percent for the company.

Sometimes we give more importance to what others say, putting aside our own criteria.

For example, a prominent physician was invited to observe their favorite sports announcer broadcast live on the radio. He was filled with excitement as the time approached. While waiting for the program to begin, he was able to observe the sports announcer and his interactions with the radio station personnel. Between live sports casting moments he appeared very hostile and condescending toward the staff. However, during live broadcasts he was a completely different person projecting warmth and support for everyone. Needless to say, the physician's impression of him was forever changed.

Somewhere along the way during this sports announcer's career, he came to believe that the key to success is through power, intimidation and the like. Instead, a more positive way of thinking might be that "you can attract more flies with honey than with vinegar."

It is up to us to choose the alternative. We can choose to handle our emotions and attitudes toward situations that arise, regardless of the roles we play within our companies.

It is we who have the control over attitudes. We can make them generate positive results, or we can allow them to manage us negatively, forming chains that in time become like rock crystal. It is difficult to break these mental chains, and they can drive us to the point of losing our objectivity.

Remember, we are reproducers of the attitudes that we assume.

- **The Opportunity**

  In conclusion, if we decide to apply our words with love in all areas, the words will help us change our thinking, the way we communicate, and what we project. Therefore, it will be reflected in our actions, generating new opportunities with each one of the people, circumstances, and places where and with whom we find ourselves.

Chapter 3

A Job That Makes Me Happy

- **Journey or Destination**

Have you ever heard someone say, "I want a job that makes me happy"? Generally, when you start working at your first assignment or opportunity, your enthusiasm is great. You have a high level of motivation, and joy and a desire to do everything right. You feel comfortable in your role within the company and give your best effort in everything you attempt.

If someone asks, "How do you feel about your new job?" you might answer, "Perfect. It is a wonderful company." And, of course, you would describe it in detail to the last corner of the building, including your work area. You might continue to talk about the people with whom you have interacted, beginning with, "My boss and my coworkers are incredible," and finish with the words, "I feel happy."

As time passes, often only a few months, some people start with the process of discontent. They begin by criticizing different aspects of the job, such as, the little work that others do in comparison to what they do, the schedule, the supervisor, the boss, the owner, the salary, the physical environment, the cafeteria, and more, finally finishing with the words, "I do not feel happy in this job."

Some people continue in the same company with the same criticism for a long time, years in some cases. They perform their work generally well but create a negative environment, one of nonconformity. They even manage to integrate other people into this negative environment and to infect them with their attitude of discontent.

Other times, people look for another job opportunity, they find it, and then after a period of happiness, they begin the same circle of criticism until they reach the same conclusion: "I do not feel happy in this work."

In the first place, let us remember that eventually the satisfaction we feel with any job changes. The things we possess, the circumstances, the events, and even for what was today a great achievement, change. We change, and life and everything around us changes.

If we identify and attach our happiness to things, people, events, or achievements, when do we believe we are going to achieve happiness? The choice to seek and find happiness is in the place where it truly resides: within ourselves.

• Justifying Your Reasoning

The second thing I ask myself is, at the moment of choosing our work, do we do it thinking: What do we really want to do? What are our aspirations for this new job? If the tasks are to our liking, what do we expect from the company? What opportunity do we have to be promoted? At the moment, when we are presented with the option to work, do we accept it by necessity, for attractive economic remuneration, or because we have not worked for a long time?

A student who was working their way through college had a job in a restaurant. He worked his way up into a management position where the money was lucrative. He didn't really care for this type of work but because of the good salary, he let his studies fall behind. He even cut his course load in half. Then one day the restaurant owners announced that they were closing and all were terminated. This was a shock for him as he realized the mistake that was made by neglecting his studies and losing his focus for money. After a little while, the new owners called and offered him a management position with a greater salary than before and he leaped at the opportunity. Again, as time passed, his studies were neglected.

Sometimes we don't learn from our mistakes. Instead, we allow events to repeat.

So if we analyze this situation, in many cases it is not the companies where we work, our positions, salaries, coworkers, bosses, supervisors, or work locations that are the culprits leading to dissatisfaction. Instead it may be our choices when we are looking for work, a lifestyle or that which is within ourselves that makes us continue with the same pattern for years and years.

- **Analyzing**

  - What if, instead of criticizing in a destructive way, we looked for a way to help constructively?

  - How many times can we blame situations, people, or things for what we lack?

  - Imagine what would happen if we looked inside ourselves, analyzed what kind of crystal chains we have (e.g., anger, jealousy, judgmental, gossip, etc.), and looked first at making a personal change instead of expecting the people around us to change?

• **Prospecting**

If for some reason you do not feel happy in your work, analyze what is happening. If it is your job that needs to change, help to get this done, but do the work with enthusiasm, giving the best of yourself professionally and personally.

You chose to work in that company; be grateful for it, for your position, for the salary you receive, and for each part of the organization. Do not expect anyone to tell you that you are doing the right thing. It is your responsibility to do your job well every time. You do not need supervision or anyone else complimenting your work at every turn.

Furthermore, if you are the one who wants to change and decide to look for another job opportunity because your professional expectations, salary, and/or environment are different from what you hoped for, you are most likely going to find it elsewhere. Leaving the company where you are currently working gives an opportunity to another person to occupy the position you have been performing.

And if you are looking for work or want to become independent, do not allow yourself to develop crystal chains (negative thoughts and attitudes). You are better off looking for those options where you see yourself fully, doing what you want, what you like, and what contributes to your peace and tranquility.

Happiness is inside of you. You have it, and it is your treasure!

Chapter 4

Deaf Ears

- ## Two Ears and One Mouth

  It is very common to hear that we have one mouth and two ears, which implies that we should listen more and talk less, as stated by Zeno of Citium. It is rare that in our daily lives, in any scenario and even more in the workplace, that we follow this premise, a premise that would lead us to have very good interpersonal relationships.

  Listening attentively shows an interest in what others express. We understand what they say to us, and we can ask questions if something is not clear. We can even give the correct answer, if necessary, on the subject.

- **Matters of the Ego**

  When another person does not listen, does not want to listen, or only listens to certain individuals, we generally imply that our conversations are falling on deaf ears. This generates disagreements and can become controversial between those who wish to give their opinions and those who are not heard.

  To stop listening and believe that we are the only ones who are right in everything can become habitual, and it discounts the ideas of others. These ideas might be the ones that provide solutions to challenging situations. In addition, without realizing it, we may be discounting people in front of their colleagues, thus making them feel that their ideas are ridiculous or unimportant.

  In these scenarios, it is the ego that is in command, and it is the ego that causes us to make these errors in judgment.

- **Farewell to Opportunities**

  With this attitude, you can miss out on great opportunities. For example, if someone has an idea that would have financial benefits, but knows from past experiences what happens when others give suggestions, he or she might remain silent. Or, because of rumors, if someone believes his or her suggestions will be rejected, he or she might remain silent. They will simply cast their ideas aside and continue with what they do in their daily lives, lest they become subject to embarrassment or ridicule in front of others.

Remaining silent results in lost opportunities, such as recognition, better income, promotions, and more.

- **Breaking Communication**

Asking the opinion of or requesting help from the boss is sometimes necessary. It does not matter if the answer is, "I do not know," or "Let me investigate." The important thing is that the person feels that it was addressed.

What do we think or how do we act if someone makes a mistake? If we are enraged, we do not listen. If we make the mistake out to be the end of the world, we are unprofessional. Making comments about others in an unprofessional manner only compounds the situation. Do you think the next time a challenge presents itself, you will find out what happened, or will they try to hide it from you?

Let us evaluate if it is the lack of, or incorrect communication, that is the origin for several of the crystal chains that we have possibly created in ourselves, and with others, that will affect our working life.

If so, we are breaking an essential part of our relationships, which will allow us to be more competitive, achieve goals, and contribute to a good organizational climate.

- **Target Shooting**

  We can create with our attitudes, words, and actions that others do not receive our ideas, even though, our ideas may be brilliant.

  Let's challenge ourselves in our thinking. What are we thinking and how do we want to express our thoughts before we speak? How do we answer and what attitude do we assume, no matter how small or large the problem?

  The phrases we use when giving opinions are important. If we are solving a problem, the words we choose can make others believe that we do not want to get involved (even if we have the solution in our hands). Instead, we can convey that we really are interested in helping to get the solution.

If we are complaining about everything around us or the behavior of our co-workers, how do we expect others to react when we talk about something that really matters?

If at any time we need to complain, let's do it professionally. Let's talk about the specific problem with the right person by focusing on the situation.

If we commit to doing something and we fail to fulfill that commitment, it decreases the chances that next time they will believe or listen. If we say we are going to do something, we need to follow through with our words and be committed with responsibility.

So, therefore, let us listen attentively and receive messages well. We should have actions consistent with our words. This is the key to winning when it comes to communicating.

- **The Exception to the Rule**

There are certain situations, where having "deaf ears" is beneficial to individuals and groups. For example, when we hear rumors and hurtful comments about people or the organization. Giving our opinion may not have not any effect on the situation, and the desired result will not be achieved. The most valuable characteristic for us is to be masters of our silence and not slaves of our words.

- **Destroying the Chain**

  If we listen actively and assertively, we will be breaking the crystal chains of having "deaf ears" and gain benefits, such as respect for others, reduced tension, individual growth, clarity, and, above all, the feeling of expressing ourselves with true freedom.

Chapter 5

Power Hungry

- **Craving Power**

The ego and the need to win are so strong and so ingrained in some people that they do not imagine the harm they are causing themselves, or others. They are indifferent to all others in order to achieve what they want in their roles.

This crystal chain is easy to find in any circumstance of life, regardless of education, culture, economic level, or position. In addition, these cravings can arise in all situations where the desire for authority, control, domination, and winning makes people do anything to achieve this power.

- **Near You**

  The craving for power often starts in families, between siblings, cousins, and parents. If this environment is created at the core of our society, what do you think will happen later in life?

  If we look within the normal areas of work, do you believe that within this environment there also exists this craving for power? Have you experienced it or been a witness?

  Have some people used it to get ahead? They often have lost the real objective. Instead, they are dominating and controlling and influence others who are not as strong and do not feel capable of resisting. This leads them to lose sight of what is important and real.

- **Stepping Strong**

  When the craving for power dominates everything you do, you may lie, criticize, and exaggerate small mistakes people make, regardless of how easily they may be fixed. You might disrespect others with your actions or words. You tend not to share knowledge with others. These are the types of people who believe they know everything and therefore do not work as a team. In general, these individuals turn people away instead of leading by example.

In addition, other strategies are used to achieve power, such as doing everything the boss tells them even if they know that is not the correct solution. It also leads them to accuse others and to create confrontations until they divide and/or destroy relationships. Simply put, they stomp their feet, not because of virtuous intentions, but because they can step on whatever or whoever is in their way.

- **A Dignified Retirement**

We sometimes see in various occupations that people who cling to power believe that after so many years, they continue to perform at peak efficiency. Despite the facts showing them that it is time to retire, they continue with their mediocre work performance. They prevent other people with different knowledge and ideas from filling the position.

It's almost as if they prefer that the company declines in performance, rather than admit their ideas are no longer correct or represent the best for the organization. They do not want to give up this power. Power blinds the real objectives of growth of the person and their quality of life. It does not let them understand that it is better to leave a good impression of an impeccable career, than to exit leaving bitter tastes in peoples' mouths.

- **The True Leader**

It is very different if we are focused on the power of leadership. The true leader directs, guides, provides confidence, makes sound decisions, sets high goals, and encourages others to successfully achieve company goals. If there are misunderstandings, they clarify any conflicts with those involved, showing respect and creating a good working environment.

The true leader creates opportunities and helps others achieve growth within the company, solve problems, and build solutions. They work as a team, listen to suggestions, and get others to listen and understand. They share knowledge, and if at any time do not know the issue, they admit it and, if necessary, ask for help.

If true leaders need to give reprimands, they do it privately when they are calm. They do not need to raise their voices or say things that can hurt other people. The true leader offers guidance and communicates clearly even while reprimanding.

In addition, true leaders are willing to change, are sensitive to the difficulties of others, and have a sense of humor. They know their strengths and weaknesses. They are productive and responsible and generally work from the basis of values, respect, creativity, and service. These are the reasons why true leaders have followers.

Chapter 6

Manipulating Puppets

- ## Since Childhood

We learned to manipulate, without knowing that we were doing it, since childhood. When we cried and kicked for an ice cream, a toy, or anything else, we got the attention of our parents, brothers, or relatives. We knew perfectly well that with the tantrum we got what we wanted; that is, with our attitude, we made others think and act the way we chose at a given moment.

- ## Manipulating Managers

One way to achieve results may be to manipulate an idea or situation where a person or a group behaves and thinks in the same way. Many times, this manipulation can get good results, other times disastrous, and at other times, nothing at all. Manipulation can be created for different purposes, and what is good for some, may not be for others. At different moments of our lives, without consciously knowing, we have manipulated others or allowed ourselves to be manipulated.

For example, a president of a company had three sales representatives who performed very well. So well, that they were promoted to positions as managers. Each of these managers were now in charge of several sales representatives. As time passed, these managers became lazy and unproductive, however, they were able to hide this fact from the president through means of manipulation of the people below. This was accomplished by favors, loans, time off, etc. Eventually the sales representatives became dissatisfied and left one-by-one. They were replaced with new personnel and the cycle of manipulation continued.

Think about manipulation affects our marital relationships, politics, advertising, fashion, economy, friendships, society, and the companies where we work.

- **Acting Like Puppets**

  At work, we can find that there are always people who let themselves be manipulated and do everything to gain the boss's favor. These people let themselves be used for any reason that is requested, regardless of their feelings about if it is right or wrong, or if they agree. They do these things because they want to gain favor in someone's eyes or they're afraid to refuse the request. They sometimes receive unwarranted praise or congratulations in front of their co-workers. The praise may also include bonuses or a special greeting from the boss that is usually reserved for puppets.

  This behavior sometimes results in resentment from co-workers instead of getting the support to achieve the objectives of the company. This will often generate conflicts between co-workers, and they might not give their best effort in their work. In addition, valuable time is lost due to co-workers gossiping about the puppet instead of focusing on their tasks. Workplace mistakes can often be the end result.

  In more extreme cases, these puppets become a part of the managerial organization. This can discourage others who believed that they could advance in the organization entirely on their own merits and job performance.

- **Manipulation is Not the Same as Influence**

Manipulation is in no way positive, since it subtly controls a group of people or a situation and prevents free development.

It is a crystal chain that can be easily broken by realizing that we are being manipulated, and any result that is achieved from this lack of free development is harmful to both us, and society.

It is different to be an influential person who respects the free will of others. Generally, the influential person feels professionally safe, and therefore, is not threatened by people with different ideas. They understand others can have good contributions to the organization, and they consider them valued members of a team.

True leaders give others recognition for good results achieved with their contributions to the managers and their colleagues, creating an environment where the working group truly wants to bring forth new ideas because they believe in their leader.

Furthermore, if true leaders find a situation where they disagree because they believe that the idea does not contribute to the objectives of the company, they should defend their position with respect, professionalism, and ethics.

They also let their peers and their managers know about these disagreements, since they are able to communicate, listen, and share their ideas. They are able to learn from the ideas of others as well. They have the ability to say "yes" or "no" when necessary. These people see equality in all human beings. They know that they are fulfilling a role in the company. They fulfill it with responsibility and honesty, and it is with that same responsibility and honesty that they treat others. This achieves the collaboration of everyone and therefore the objectives of their department, and the company as a whole can be a success.

- **Making Way**

In conclusion, human beings are differentiated by the decisions they make, and it is their actions that define them and demonstrate, who they are in different stages of life.

Chapter 7

On Time

- **What Defines Us**

To arrive on time is to be at the right moment when an event occurs, or to arrive at the appointed time when we have a commitment.

In turn, it can be defined as a discipline and endows our personality with character, order, and effectiveness that therefore somehow define us. It also means valuing, considering, and respecting the time of other people.

However, there is always an excuse for not doing so, which can become a bad habit and over time a crystal chain that ties us and weighs us down.

- **Justifying Us**

  There are different excuses to justify any situation when we are accustomed to being late, not only to an appointment or to our work, but to all parts for which we have created a series of excuses that we use with an abysmal tranquility.

  Depending on the person(s) or circumstances, we can cite as an excuse: the traffic, the car (a tire was damaged or the car did not start), the weather (it was raining or hot), the alarm did not ring, the previous appointment went over time, I have too much work, my children's school, the teacher, my boss, among others. We even sometimes go over the limit by giving as an excuse the health of a loved one.

  And often, even in the same location, we are late to a meeting where we need only to move two or three doors, and we make excuses like a last-minute e-mail, the computer system, the printer, or a phone call.

- **The Value of Punctuality**

  Reliability generates tranquility and confidence. It also demonstrates professionalism, organization, commitment, good planning, courtesy, and respect for others.

Managing time is important, not only arriving at the agreed upon time, but also the way we spend that precious gift called time.

We have already discussed in previous paragraphs some aspects that others can perceive and some that are generated in us when we have control of our time. To use it in an optimal way, we must have skills, such as organization and planning, that will help us.

We can find excellent plans that do not work, not because of the planning itself, but because when executing the plan, time became secondary or insignificant.

When we do not manage our time correctly, we can miss opportunities to grow professionally.

Think of a professional who does his or her job impeccably but consistently delivers it after the agreed-upon time. It may be that the company has the desire to promote someone with the professional profile of this person. Do you think they would promote this person, given the opportunity to fill a new position? It may be that they believe the individual's knowledge base is excellent for the job, but that he or she has no time-management skills and that this affects the work group, and therefore, the company.

If, on the other hand, this person manages his or her time and is punctual, that makes everyone trust the person and trust that he or she will do what needs to be done to achieve all the commitments made. Now, the possibility of occupying a new position within the company and growing professionally has been increased.

- **Commitment**

We all commit ourselves, either with the family, in school, in sports, or at work. Sometimes we sign contracts that we understand and others where the understanding is not so clear. A commitment may contain something implicit that goes further than what was agreed upon in writing, such as being courteous to co-workers.

It is like an engine that moves and can be perceived in many ways, one of which can be when you do or execute a project or work in a shorter time than expected. Or many times, when this commitment pushes us, we may even be surprised, because we are doing more than expected at the same time.

But the commitment that is acquired goes beyond the word and manifests itself with facts: If you say you will do it, do it! If not, do not say that you will because the proof is in the deeds, not words.

There was a sales representative at a trade show displaying their product when a foreign buyer approached the booth. He wanted to know what their company offered that was better than the competition whose prices were more appealing. Without hesitation the sales representative answered "we have a 24/7 service call system." The foreign buyer was interested and thanked them for the information. He went away from the booth and made a phone call to the 24/7 system and was placed on hold for an extended period of time. Needless to say, the company missed out on a great selling opportunity because they couldn't deliver on their promise.

- **Watching the Clock**

Another important topic is how we use our time in the workplace.

One of the most frequent practices in companies is that the employees leave "on time" at the end of the workday. They are getting ready a half an hour before departure. They might even stop attending to clients or avoid scheduling meetings around this time in order to leave at the agreed-upon time.

However, is this the same behavior we observe during the morning arrival times? Are we arriving half an hour before the agreed-upon time to get ready for our day? No. To the contrary, we hurry to "clock in" at the hour without hesitation, and then we dedicate the next several minutes of the morning hour getting ready. We may turn on the computer, greet each other, go to the restroom, get a cup of coffee, and check e-mails.

Similarly, at lunchtime, do we take allotted time or do we extend the lunch hour? In the same manner, we can evaluate the time we use to take a break in the morning or mid-afternoon.

This does not even include the time invested in personal calls or visits with co-workers, time reviewing social networks, personal e-mails, and chat rooms.

So, how much time are we actually working versus the hours spent at work for which we are hired and paid our wages?

• Looking for Answers

Do we use our work schedule with responsibility?

Each of us must answer this question according to how we believe we are acting, not by what others say or by what the boss or supervisor has seen.

This is something so personal that only with honesty can we have the right answer.

Being on time speaks to the person we are and demonstrates some personality traits we exhibit. If improper use of time is our crystal chain, we are on time to break it if we wish.

Chapter 8

Respecting

- **Day after Day**

  Thousands and thousands of people spend much of their lives in the workplace. They make companies thrive with the work they do each day. As leaders (directors, managers, and supervisors), we are in the position to help create and maintain a good working environment.

  A vital part is the way we communicate. It often becomes so routine that we do not believe it makes a difference.

  It is through these types of communication (verbal and non-verbal) that we have in our day-to-day interactions with people that we may generate a different environment.

- **Communicating**

  Let us ask ourselves:

  - Have we ever been in a bad mood or have we reacted in an inappropriate way for something we did not want to do?

  - Do we believe that we are right, because we are "numero uno" regardless of the circumstance or the place?

  - Do we not take the time to care for others because we are always too busy?

  - Do we speak loudly to be heard and for others to know who we are when we do not agree with something or someone?

  - Do we make inappropriate comments about our colleagues or the people we are managing when they are not present?

  - Are we always competing with others, so it is difficult to accept the ideas and cooperation of others?

  When we choose one of these positions, we are not gaining anything; we just want to be right and be the first in everything.

- **Winning or Imposing**

  With poor communication and inappropriate behavior, we believe we win the respect of others, but in reality, we are imposing. It is often out of necessity or fear that some people put up with our behavior.

  Out of Necessity?

  Some people use the term "necessity" to describe their work, since they should or must work in whatever it takes to earn a salary to support themselves and/or their family. For them, work becomes a necessity. Their wants do not prevail, nor do their goals or dreams. They really do want to work on what they desire. Since the first link in their scale of priorities is to meet basic needs, this does not give them the time to choose. They simply choose to be employed, and if it is in the shortest possible amount of time spent doing it, all the better.

  These are the people who very possibly do not agree with many forms of communication or behavior that are used with them, but because the need to keep a job is their one and only priority, this is what makes them remain silent and tolerate everything, including things with which they disagree.

Out of Fear?

In some situations, people create fear with their immense egos, by verbally berating or embarrassing, speaking loudly, or ignoring others.

If we experience fear, so strong that we are paralyzed without knowing how to respond or what to do when the other person's behavior is unreasonable or by a situation in our work, let us ask: What is the maximum we can lose? What would happen, if with respect, we discussed it with the person and gave our point of view?

• Distorting Reality

By contrast, is it we who are irritated? If it is we who want to dominate the situation and be "numero uno", stop and consider if the ideas that other people are presenting are good. If they are good and would contribute to the objectives of the organization and we are not allowing them because of our ego, we need to re-evaluate how we are communicating.

The ego is the mental trait most frequently used to divide and distort reality. It interferes with listening. It does not take into account the ideas of others. It wants to rule the world, no matter the consequences, solely with the goal of winning. If we use it frequently in our lives, what are we gaining from this attitude? Maybe we can temporarily believe that we have achieved everything, but over time, we come to realize it is not reality.

In some situations, we simply watch without the need to win, and the result is we help others win.

• Underlying Tension

I once heard in the hallways of a company, "There is a silence that is deafening," and they were serious!

Prolonged silence often persists between the employees and employers despite the knowledge that portions of communication have been broken and relationships have deteriorated. They prefer to keep quiet and carry on. This is because one of the most important pillars in relationships, respect, has been lost. Communication has been compromised, but both parties need one another for the company to function and to continue solving problems.

• Thinking before Speaking

For many years, we have heard the saying, "Think before speaking and don't speak before thinking."

If before addressing a person, we think about what we are going to say and how we are going to present it, we will probably avoid many unpleasant situations.

If, on the contrary, we answer or we address them angrily, afterward, we might think, If only I had said X, Y, or Z. We cannot take back the words we speak or the possible harm we create.

It is up to us alone to break this portion of the crystal chain. Sometimes situations dictate that we say a certain thing at the moment, but it might be inappropriate, so it is better to wait and speak at another time. Our words might have been perfect, but by postponing our words for later in a different environment, feelings of others may be spared.

• The Basis of it All

In any area of our lives, respect is the foundation of every relationship we establish. Without this foundation, we can hardly build healthy relationships. This holds true in the work environment as well.

Each and every person is unique. We know that all we have to do is listen actively, that the opinions of others are as valuable as our own, and that the emotions we are feeling are differen. other people experience in the moment.

Good communication can be achieved whe. express what we feel, what we need, or what . want. This can be done without judging the person and simply saying things calmly while remaining clear and secure in ourselves.

We know that respect is not demanded or imposed. To do so would surely not achieve the expected results. Good results are consequences of the good treatment that we give others from day to day.

Chapter 9

The Magnificence of Forgiveness

- **Resentment**

When we have negative feelings from the past, our attitudes can change every time we think about the past experiences. We can get in a bad mood and have feelings of hurt and pain. For now we can call this "resentment."

Resentment is something that was generated by a situation at a given time in the past, and we rarely recognize it in the moment. This is the reason why resentment can be one of the most difficult crystal chains to break.

- **The Open Wound**

This is similar to when we have a wound that we prevent from healing. The wound is open, and we continue to pick at it and open it more and more. Over time, the wound becomes larger with more issues than we had previously. All of this is a result of not being able to confront and deal with the problem initially.

One of the things that can create a difficult work environment is finding people who have similar feelings and experiences at the company, and instead of working to resolve the issues, we consciously or unconsciously seek only people who will agree with us. This behavior serves to continue opening rather than closing the wound.

- **Errors and Opinions**

People see and think differently about people they know, especially when they are hearing conversations regarding these people. It is very important to have our own thoughts before commenting about others.

Some people remember, criticize, and fail to forgive the most insignificant errors. Many small mistakes are made at work, and those who do not make mistakes might very well be the ones who do very little. This leads them to speak badly, criticize, and accuse others. They believe that with this attitude, they are winning, when in fact, with these action they are hurting themselves.

People who harbor longstanding resentments seem to permanently live in a "bad mood." They look for ways to retaliate and make people pay for their mistakes. This can create internal tension and health problems.

• Turning the Page

Is it worth living like this for an action from the past that usually makes little sense? How many times have we lost our perspective and our present moment by bringing up past problems?

We know that we are all different and that not everyone around us agrees with what we say or do and with the decisions we make.

Maybe it's time to stop on the road and see if we resent someone and what caused this feeling, and then, solve it!

We must not wear ourselves out and waste precious time and opportunities by returning to the past and failing to move forward.

Forgiven

Just as in a moment we can generate a negative feeling, we can also generate a positive one and forgive.

We believe in the magnificence of forgiving and asking for forgiveness!

When we make a mistake, we need to have the courage to admit it and simply say, "Please forgive me," or, "Excuse me." "Can we talk about what happened and correct the situation?" Let us forgive with honesty and sincerity through our words and actions.

Let's not wait for other people to apologize or to forgive us. We can forgive ourselves! This creates a great opportunity to free ourselves of resentments and to free ourselves from harboring old feelings so that we can finally heal our wounds.

Chapter 10

Customer Service with Every Breath

- ## To Be or Not to Be

  We are all aware of one way or another that serving is one of the most precious and powerful values that life has given us.

  Serving is an attitude. It is the decision we make about how to behave with other people in a given situation.

  And it is with this service we can provide in our daily lives to others in all circumstances of life, regardless of whether we are travelling, at school, at work, in the supermarket, or on the street.

- ## What Our Customers Expect

  Generally when we think of service, we focus on the service that all companies in one way or another expect to provide to their customers or, on the service that we as clients expect to receive.

We know that service is the key, and that in most cases, the increase in sales and overall growth of the company is dependent on the attention given to our customers.

How many companies want to have excellent service for their customers? And who are these customers?

Clearly, the first answer is that all companies want to give excellent service. The second answer is customers are those who buy a product and/or service, therefore, we may ask, "What happens to the people with whom you interact every day at work?" Are they not your customers too?

If we do not see them as customers, how do we expect the company to breathe service? How then can we expect our external customers to get extraordinary service?

• Service with Quality

Years ago, I studied, analyzed, and followed the philosophy of "total quality service," which is defined in part as "the quest for continuous improvement in our organizations." One of the things that struck me most about this philosophy was that the definition for the internal and the external customer is the same: "to achieve satisfaction for the needs and expectations of the customer."

In addition, by taking the concept into our daily lives, the internal customers are all the people with whom, in one way or another, we have a relationship, therefore, we can apply this philosophy to all areas of our lives.

Hence, we achieve the objectives proposed in the organizations, generating a pleasant work environment while having the opportunity to grow.

- **Commitment**

If we really wish to take this concept of the internal customer and put it into practice where we work, we need to begin with ourselves, and the key to this beginning is: service. If we are committed to a high level of internal service within our company, this will automatically be reflected in our service to our external customers.

The level of service we expect to receive when we need help is the same service we can provide at any given time to our internal or external customers.

We decide how much we want to provide when we give service, and we always want the best. In the same manner that we expect and want it, we must provide it to others as well.

For example, a man calls a company and asks to speak to the person in charge of the human resources department stating "It is urgent." The receptionist responds cordially to the request, explaining that the person in charge is not available and will respond later. The receptionist never lets the caller give an explanation as to the urgency of his call. After some time passes, the man calls again and is transferred to an extension that rings, but no-one answers. He calls back a third time and is mistakenly transferred to still another department. The caller indicates that he has been wrongly transferred and is subsequently returned to the receptionist. Hours later, the human resources person contacts the employee's cell phone. Much to the person's surprise, the cell phone is answered by the husband of the employee, who explains that for the last hour his wife has been delivering their baby early. He further explains that he had repeatedly called to speak with the company to inform them of the situation, as he knew his wife had a very important meeting with some investors and she did not want them needlessly waiting for her. Unfortunately, he could not get the message to them.

In these particular situations, are we providing excellent service? No. We are delaying processes, hampering tasks, and losing commitments.

It would have been a "service-oriented" attitude if we had asked the caller how we could help and if he wanted to leave a message or a phone number where the call could be returned. Very likely, the message would have been returned in a timely manner without affecting customers. Both the internal (employee) and external (investors) customers were negatively affected in the above scenario.

- **Attitude and Aptitude**

People's attitudes can change when asking for help. Their attitudes are different depending on the situation they are experiencing at the moment. For example, you may be angry, which prevents you from asking the right questions, or you may raise your voice, which also prevents you from getting the help you need.

It may be that when we face this situation, we do not listen, we interrupt, we do not clarify, or we adopt a position in which we believe we know everything. We may act as though we do not know what they are talking about when we could actually be of help. No matter how big the problem, we can find a solution; it all depends on our attitude.

It is important to keep calm, to reassure ourselves, and to analyze all the aspects that we know of the situation so that the person requesting help has a satisfactory answer, feels comfortable, and is given the proper attention.

In addition, if we are in a company, it is because we have the skills to be part of this environment and therefore the skills to help the growth of the organization. And one of the most important factors for this growth is the timely attention to our customers.

• Solidarity and Equal Treatment

Some people provide various types of service depending on the individual. This may depend on whether they are the boss, a friend, or if they are tall or short.

When we really want to provide excellent service, we do the same for everyone. There are no differences! We are kind to everyone! We help solve problems, and if we do not know how, we inform the person as to where he or she may find help.

- **The Most Effective Advertising**

There will be situations where people have differences with their customers.

Let's analyze this situation. After attending to a customer with a problem, and that customer has left, the person who attended to them initiates a contemptuous conversation about the customer and the situation with their co-worker.

How will the people who are waiting for service and heard our conversation feel about the situation? Many times we may be right and the customer may be wrong, but what sense does it make to talk about that customer and what happened right then? It is better to talk to the right person at the right time, analyze the situation, and take measures so that it does not happen again.

Generally when we are in the role of customers and we hear negative comments about another customer, we think to ourselves, If they are talking like that about the customer who just left, they will talk about me the same way if I need help some day. Moreover, the customer who came out disgusted will most likely discuss this situation with other people who have nothing to do with our company, but the comments and the name of our company is etched in their minds. When the day comes that they need a product or service, they will not think of our company but rather another competing company.

Service is the most effective means of advertising in the marketplace!

• Leaving Our Comfort Zone

As we discussed at the beginning of this chapter, this concept of customer service can affect almost all the actions of our lives because we are all customers. We can apply it in our home, when we are with our partner, with our children, with friends, with people that cross our paths—that is, in any relationship.

We have the opportunity to serve without anyone asking us for help. Sometimes, the person who asks us for help, needs only to be heard, and that action in itself serves.

When we are driving and we see that another car wants to pass and we give way, or when we see a pedestrian is crossing and we stop the car until they can pass and feel safe, with these small actions we are also serving.

We can serve when we are in the restaurant and the waitress or the person who serves us does not understand what we are requesting and we repeat the request calmly and with a smile. In addition, when we speak in a low voice and create a pleasant atmosphere for our companions or for the people who are around us, we are also serving.

We can use intuition to respond to the needs of others. If necessary, let us ask ourselves, how can we help? Or, how can we serve at this moment?

In order to give this help, it is necessary to leave our "comfort zone." In other words, we must place ourselves in the shoes of others. This means offering up ourselves for the benefit of others.

If you want to do something, you can! If you do not have the resources at the moment, you still have the creativity to find help through others.

- **Flee from Indifference**

Once I noticed a girl get on a public bus in the early hours of the morning. Because it was rush hour, the bus was without any empty seats. A few stops later, a woman with a walking difficulty boarded. The girl, upon seeing the situation, interceded on her behalf by asking for help from a young man nearby to give the lady his seat. As soon as he noticed help being requested, the young man closed his eyes and pretended to be asleep. Seeing his attitude, the girl insisted again to get his attention, and he reluctantly agreed to give up his seat. Once the young man had given up his seat, the girl asked the lady if she would like to sit in order to make herself more comfortable. The lady responded in a commanding voice, "Who told you that I wanted to sit? Does it seem to you that I am an old woman that cannot stand for a ride?" The astonished girl told her, "I just thought you would be more comfortable." The lady reproached her and insulted her for several more minutes. Soon after, the young man who had given up his seat continued with the condemnation of the girl for interceding in an affair that, according to him, was none of her business. The astonished girl was confused, wondering if it was ever worth it to help.

As we can see in this example, the girl wanted to help but could not. The young man did not want to help, and the lady did not allow anyone to help.

Sometimes it is possible that although we have great intentions, we are not able to serve, but we cannot let this generate one of the most complicated crystal chains that we are facing in the world: indifference.

Surely, there will be many attempts to help, and only some will succeed in our daily lives, but the satisfaction of having served will be incalculable.

- **You Have the Power**

In short, if we fully understand the depth of the word serve and put it into practice in our lives, we will be using one of the greatest and most magnificent powers we all possess.

Questions of Attitude

- **Healthy Relationships**

  We work in harmony. It is a strategy that some companies would like to adopt and others would like to maintain. We all agree that working in an environment with good human relationships is excellent and that we are the ones who make these words ring true.

  For instance, it is good to take a look at the relationship we have with ourselves. We know that this relationship is very important and that it guides us in many aspects of our lives. So what is the relationship we have chosen with which to lead our lives? Have we learned to love ourselves? Do we forgive ourselves? Are we open to change and to breaking many of the crystal chains that bind us?

In Others' Shoes

Relationships are different between people because each person is unique. In addition, there are other factors that influence our dealings with people. These include the lifestyles of us and the other person, the cultures of our countries of origin, our experiences, our emotions, our circumstances, and our way of reacting to situations that arise. Furthermore, the interests of both parties, the level of empathy, our views on life, and the titles or positions that we occupy within the company have an impact.

Let us also remember that each person has his or her own history on different levels (personal, family, work and spiritual). We do not know the history of the other person and the difficulties or situations the person has experienced.

Therefore, we cannot make judgments about others. Instead, we might place ourselves in the shoes of the other person, if even for a single instant, without judging.

- **Criticizing**

At work, it's amazing to see how often we inadvertently get involved in destructive criticism about others in order to feel part of a group. In addition, we lack the courage to say what we think or challenge the situation, again, in order to remain part of the group.

For example, despite remaining silent and not asking the right questions to clarify what others are saying during a meeting, we embark on a post-meeting critique of everything that happened with others. Instead of saying the things that we disagree with at the meeting, we choose to mimic, mock, and put down not only the ideas of other people, but the people themselves.

We sometimes talk on the phone for a long time, and after we hang up, with our actions we imply that the conversation was not interesting, though when we were talking, we seemed very interested in the subject. We speak badly of our phone contact without thinking that we were also involved in that conversation.

We meet with some colleagues to share a moment of rest, and the topic of conversation becomes criticizing the others or the company in which we are working, and none of the people in the group dare to change the conversation, make a constructive criticism, defend, or simply say, "I do not agree."

In all of these situations, criticism dominates. What would happen if we instead talked to the person and gave him or her the opportunity to state his or her point of view? What need do we have to be in a meeting where the comments we make, place the other in an uncomfortable position?

- **Negative Criticism**

  Negative criticism is contagious. Yes, very contagious! It is like an illness, and we are unaware of the damage it causes to us and to others. In our companies, we sometimes use it to get better positions, to be part of the group, or to find a way to make others lose.

- **Positive Criticism**

  If we use criticism in a constructive way by looking for ways to help people with their ideas, we contribute to the objectives of our company. By meeting these universal objectives, we maintain good relationships between employees, work as a team, and enjoy a pleasant working atmosphere.

- **An Issue of Respect**

  Respect is basic to maintaining good interpersonal relationships. It is not necessary to impose our views if we do not agree with the other person's opinion on a specific topic. This does not mean that we must hide our point of view or that we do not talk about ways to improve.

  On the contrary, it is essential that we contribute our ideas. We know that we can often contribute something that may improve the way we do our work, and sometimes the work of others.

- **The Attitude**

  We understand attitude as the means of acting or behaving with others using verbal or non-verbal (body posture, for example) communication. When we respect the power we have with our attitude, we use it as an effective tool to help us break the crystal chains that bind us in most of our relationships.

  Our attitudes are the most important generators to the organizational climate in which we work. With our attitudes, we can transform actions, thoughts, and words. It is reflected in the way we handle the situations presented to us and in the way we react to them. It is the reflection of who we are and our way of thinking.

- **Unique Beings**

Because we are unique beings, every day is new, and every moment is a unique and valuable opportunity to learn and change!

In every moment, everything is being transformed, as we are too! What is good for us and other people today may not be tomorrow. The attitudes we take to these transformations are unique and personal.

We have the choice of making our attitudes a way of life that builds and delivers good feelings, or making our attitudes an indestructible crystal chain that ties, limits, and paralyzes us.

Chapter 12

Making the Change

- **The Perfect Excuse**

Over time, we find people who have lived immersed in their problems and concerns. These are the ones who believe that their destiny is bad and blame their poor decisions and difficulties on God, their spouse, their children, the government, the workplace, the weather, or just plain bad luck.

Each step that these people take or others take becomes something that for them is always wrong. They are always disgusted by everything, and nothing seems to satisfy them, even if they have the very best in life.

In general, how we view and think about our lives and the situations that surround us can be a "self-fulfilling prophecy." Why blame others for our circumstances or the things that we have created or done? Sometimes we use this as the perfect excuse to justify many of our behaviors, but it is not sensible or reasonable if we want to solve the situation.

If we would choose to evaluate ourselves and initiate a process of development and growth, we would then be taking steps toward a change in all areas of our lives.

- **Our Choice**

The paths we have gone through in our lives have been to learn with every step we take. It is our own decision whether we want to continue in the same path or to learn from our experiences, and then, to grow and get ahead.

Part of it is learning to live in our present moment. This moment is everything! It is the moment in which we are reading these words. Every moment is a gift. Let us live it with joy and with immense gratitude.

- **Influencing Mind Factor**

In contrast, if we see our work as a routine, then every day is the same, and we do our work out of obligation rather than pleasure and gratitude.

If the act of going to work has become a nightmare, the first thing that comes to mind when we wake up might be, another day of work. What a drag!

In that scenario, we make comments daily about the situations that are presented to us, seeing them as problematic. These may be about the traffic conditions, our mode of transportation, the weather, the road conditions (pot-holes, one versus two lanes, slow traffic lights, etc.). Several times during the day, we may refer to the elements that help us accomplish our work in a distasteful manner. We might express something about the system being slow, the chair being hard, the printer being old, or how we should have this or that. We are generating a negative attitude, which weighs heavily on us and prevents us from moving forward.

We can instead choose to change our thinking. Then we will see our work as an opportunity to grow and as something we like. The act of going to work will become something we enjoy, and when we wake, the first thing that will come to mind will be, Thank you for this new day! We will stop criticizing what we cannot change, such as the transportation system, the weather, and the streets. Our words will be positive, thankful, prosperous, and abundant.

- **Our Actions**

  We will get nothing from reading the best books or attending spectacular conferences with the best motivators or being at the best work meetings or going to annual company parties if we feel that we are working in an environment of mistrust, criticism, fear, and poor communication. Instead, we are just feeding the binding crystal chain of "no change."

  If we enjoyed our present moment and used it doing our work in the best way possible and enjoyed our relationships with others, the environment we find ourselves in would be completely different.

  Do not wait for the company, your co-workers, the system, or your boss to change. Start by generating a change within yourself. If we change, the whole environment automatically changes.

Gratitude

- **Defining**

  Gratitude is the feeling and recognition that a person has toward someone who has done him or her a favor or has rendered a service. Showing appreciation is the manifestation of this feeling.

- **Being Grateful**

  We often let life become a routine of coming and going through the world without enjoying or appreciating what we have at the time. These things can be as simple as our physical health or the ability to read, interpret, and understand these words in our own way.

  Sometimes we assume that the people around us know that we are totally grateful for what they do for us. We let the days pass by and do not tell them or manifest our gratitude in any way. We should know that all we might need to say is, "Thank you," "Thank you for being there for me," "Thank you for opening the door," "Thank you for giving me a glass of water," "Thank you for sharing the day with me," or, "Thank you for that phone call."

- **Restorative Process**

Is it a big deal to say "thank you?" Yes, it's a big deal to be thankful for everything.

To give thanks is an act that people do with freedom. We give thanks to ourselves and to the people around us because we appreciate what someone did for us, whether big or small. We may give thanks because we always find what we want or need. We may give thanks for the wonders we have around us or for the material things that give us comfort. We may give thanks for our bodies. Finally, we can even give thanks for the people who designed the clothes we wear.

Finally, we can be grateful for the conditions in which we live at this time. We can be grateful because we respect and love ourselves unconditionally. We can be grateful because we are able to apologize when we make mistakes and because we can learn from our mistakes.

- **Our Environment**

People do a job, and companies give them a reward for the work done. This implies that both workers and employers have a series of obligations and responsibilities between themselves. In general, this is the relationship between the two parties, including a number of laws, rights, and regulations that are in force, depending on the nature of the work, the country, and so on.

Sounds a bit cold, don't you think? It is as if we only see our company as a cold entity with an XYZ name that fulfills and enforces a series of obligations. Do you think we could really expect something different from XYZ?

Companies are created by people who want to get ahead with their investment ideas and are also made up of those who work for these people. We are located in different areas within the organization, according to our skill sets, and day by day, we do everything necessary to succeed in our tasks. We might do this in the same manner as great chefs prepare cuisines. They carefully place the exact amount of ingredients to give the perfect flavor. They serve it in a way as to give it the most spectacular presentation at the table so that the person has the opportunity to enjoy a delicious dish.

There are a few people who have the idea that if they work at a company, they only need to ask and they will achieve success without any effort. We often hear them say, "They owe us (this or that)."

- **Benefits**

Part of the success in our work, besides knowing how to do the work with responsibility, comes from enjoying it and doing it with enthusiasm. We should work as a team and with commitment. Do you think we can succeed if we use and apply the above ideas? Of course we can achieve our objectives!

Let's consider another situation. Let's suppose we do not have a job, and every day we wait for a call for an interview. After each day that passes, we hope that one of the companies where we have requested a job chooses us so that we can have the opportunity to return to work. When we finally find a new job, we are so grateful, and then what happens with time? We forget to be grateful.

How about we add a few drops of gratitude to our daily lives! If you have not added this concept to your daily thoughts, it does not mean you cannot succeed. Indeed, we see and hear of thousands of people every day that succeed, and we do not know if they added "thank you" to their comments. Surely, if you do add gratitude into your life, the benefits you see will multiply with abundance.

- **More Happiness**

When we say thank you, we express one of the greatest feelings we possess. But if we do say it, let's say it with sincerity. Do not do it simply to be compliant.

Grateful people are very happy with what life has given them. They focus on what they have, not on what they need, and most of their expectations are easily achieved.

- **Awareness**

There are so many things we can be thankful for; the list goes on forever. Be thankful for your health. We often take for granted that which we have, until the moment we are at risk of losing it or suffer an illness. We fail to give it the real value and thanks it deserves.

So it is with our intelligence too! This very thing we use every moment of our lives often goes unnoticed. Because we are so used to having it, we do not contemplate the need to say "thank you" for it.

What a gift it is to be able to say "thank you" for our work, for our colleagues, for the salary we receive, for the company where we work, and for its owners.

Let us say "thank you" for those moments that are difficult and for those that are good and extraordinary as well. Undoubtedly, the difficult ones offer us the greatest learning opportunities and help us grow. Therefore, we can always find a thousand reasons to say "thank you."

We can even say "thank you" for the ability to recognize the crystal chains that bind us and for the opportunity to change. Life gives us opportunities to free ourselves from these crystal chains by breaking them. Being grateful strengthens all our interpersonal relationships and makes us aware.

Chapter 14

The Decision

Throughout the chapters in this book, we have seen how we are influencing ourselves to live a pleasant life of personal and professional growth. We also emphasized how each person is an important piece in that puzzle we call the workplace, no matter what position we occupy.

In turn, we saw that we are the only ones who can make the decision to do things well and in a different way: performing our work with responsibility, contributing ideas, creating, sharing our knowledge with our colleagues, and respecting and giving credit to the right person(s). In other words, doing our work consciously.

Before summarizing the topics we have discussed here, I want to emphasize that you are the only person who can break the crystal chains that bind you. This is your choice in life; therefore, the only one who can take the first step and continue to reach your goal is you!

- We have read that it is valuable to stop and look at what we are doing with our lives. Many times, we do not realize that over the years we have developed habits that limit us in our personal growth. The only person that can evaluate what those crystal chains are in all sincerity is us.

- Let us also remember that by adding a few drops of love to everything we do and to the different moments we live, we give a different touch to our lives by surrounding ourselves with tranquility. What we receive in any scenario will yield different results from those without the few drops.

- We know that in many cases it is not the companies, the positions, or the circumstances that are causes for why people do not feel happy and calm in their work. Usually we choose what we want to do for work, how we want to feel, how we handle our present moment, and how we decide to live in the present moment.

- We learned the importance of communication. We learned that our body position says much about what we want to communicate. We also learned that the first thing about communication is to listen, so as to know what the other person really means before giving an answer. When we interrupt communication, we are breaking one of the essential foundations of interpersonal relations, which is basic to the organizational climate.

- We learned that sometimes the ego and the need to win are so great that we do not comprehend the damage we are doing to ourselves and other people. The craving for power does not produce good results, or give us peace of mind. It is very different when we are focused on being leaders, creating opportunities for the growth of others and therefore achieving the objectives of the company.

- We have learned that in organizations, you can see that the power of manipulation can break the values and norms society has created and that sometimes people allow themselves to play this game. We learned that things are completely different when we adopt leadership traits that respect the free will of others. Along the way, we will meet people who, with their ideas and their work, will help us in our growth.

- One of the crystal chains that we can easily define is the one where we always have excuses or the right answers as to why we cannot complete our commitments on time. In the same manner, we also realized that we might not be using our working hours responsibly.

- We stated that respect in any area of our lives is fundamental in our relationship with ourselves and with others. Without this foundation, we can hardly build healthy relationships, and the workplace environment is no exception.

- We emphasized that forgiveness is one of the greatest powers we possess. It is a great opportunity to free ourselves, to release, to heal the wounds, and to lighten the load of others and ourselves from harboring these feelings.

- We are also aware, in one way or another, that service is one of the most precious values that life has given. Serving is an attitude. It is the way we act in any one moment for the benefit of others.

- We can help maintain an organizational climate of harmony with our attitude and by having good relationships with others. This will be reflected in the achievement of the objectives of the company. Our lives generally reflect what we think about them, and the situations that surround us.

- Sometimes it is easier to blame others or circumstances for what we have done or are doing. In some situations, we can even put on a dramatic scene. We may scream, display a bad temper, or even say statements such as, "Why don't you believe me?" We handle the situation as if it were personal and even disrespect others without taking the time to wait a few seconds before reacting. We are the owners of our thoughts. If we change them, our moment changes, and therefore, our lives change.

- Being thankful is a fundamental part of a person's life. When we say "thank you," we are expressing gratitude for something that is or was good for us at any given time. Grateful people are very happy with what life has given them. They focus on what they have, not on what they need, and all their expectations are easily achieved.

Finally, the best thing we can do in any area and moment of our lives is to laugh. It is the best therapy. It frees us from the worries of life and helps us to see it for what it is, a game where we all are players.

Laughter is our friend. It is free and gives us encouragement and life. It is contagious, and with it, we feel free.

Let us laugh and share the happiness we have, giving thanks for being here at this time. Let us laugh at the mistakes we make. Let us laugh at absolutely everything because we will always have another chance to reinvent ourselves and to break the crystal chains that keep us from growing.

Thank you for the time you devoted to reading these words and pondering the many elements of our daily lives.

Angela Cook

Angela Cook is a business manager with more than forty years of experience in various disciplines of the labor industry. These include financial banking security and strategic planning, governmental data systems, and business education. Her emphasis is on strategic planning and development, staff training, and leadership, and total quality control.

She firmly believes that we can all do what we set out to do in life. Her orientation in life is directed to the only thing we really have—the present moment.

The influences from authors of motivational books and her gratitude to those who have served as her mentors and co-workers led her to take up this new challenge, the publication of her first book.

Cristina Monroy

Christina Monroy is a marketing specialist and publicist with more than twenty years of experience in different business sectors, where she has served as management in customer service, marketing, advertising, and commercial and internal auditing.

One of her life goals is to enhance the value of the human being in any area of its development. She believes that by creating synergy between different teams, our goals can be achieved.

She considers that in the different areas of life, communication is fundamental in all its forms of expression. These communication fundamentals are the main motivations for one of the activities she enjoys most—writing.